· MARY FORD ·

HOME BAKING

— WITH —

CHOCOLATE

WITH EASY STEP-BY-STEP RECIPES

2

Acknowledgements

Mary Ford acknowledges with grateful thanks the assistance of R & W Scott Ltd of Carluke in supplying all the chocolate and recipes used in this book, and all the help given by Jacqueline James in making the products.

Other Mary Ford Titles

101 CAKE DESIGNS
ANOTHER 101 CAKE DESIGNS
A CAKE FOR ALL SEASONS
CHILDREN'S CAKES
CHOCOLATE COOKBOOK
DECORATIVE SUGAR FLOWERS FOR CAKES
JAMS, CHUTNEYS AND PICKLES
MAKING CAKES FOR MONEY
MAKING GLOVE PUPPETS

MAKING SOFT TOYS
MAKING TEDDY BEARS
PARTY CAKES
SUGAR FLOWERS CAKE DECORATING
SUGARCRAFT CAKE DECORATING
SUGARPASTE CAKE DECORATING
THE COMPLETE BOOK OF CAKE DECORATING
THE CONCISE BOOK OF
CAKE MAKING AND DECORATING

1991 Mary Ford Publications Limited. Published by Mary Ford Publications Limited, 294b Lymington Road, Highcliffe on Sea, Christchurch, Dorset BH23 5ET, England.

ISBN 0 946429 33 2

Printed and bound in Hong Kong

Author

Despite spending her professional life cooking, Mary Ford has always enjoyed home baking. A naturally talented cook and an expert cake decorator, she has experimented with traditional English cookery and is expanding her interest into other areas, as indicated by the wide range of Mary Ford step-by-step craft titles.

Mary has many years of experience in cake making and her step-by-step books are known throughout the world as a unique method of passing on her skills. Her enthusiasm for teaching students, together with her own natural warmth, has endeared her to a generation of students and has ensured her a permanent place in their affections.

Mary's tremendous energy is now being channelled into bringing her skills to the widest possible audience. In partnership with her husband Michael, they are continually striving to improve the presentation of her books. Michael is the artistic director for all Mary's books and each title represents a happy and harmonious collaboration between them. Mary is responsible for preparing the products, and Michael acting as editor and co-ordinator for the book production.

Contents

Note: All the recipes in this book can be made with either Baker's chocolate, such as Scotbloc, or Couverture chocolate, such as Chocolat. Recipes always state if tempering is required when using Chocolat.

When making any of the recipes in this book, follow one set of measurements only as they are not interchangeable.

Introduction

For versatility and appeal, nothing beats the sensuousness of chocolate. Its wickedly seductive taste is irresistible to old and young alike and in this exciting new book I have chosen dozens of sumptuous but simple recipes using Scotbloc or Scotts Chocolat which are guaranteed to satisfy the most exacting chocolate enthusiast's palate. Using Scotbloc is so easy that even the most inexperienced cook will achieve perfect results.

The easy-to-follow pictorial format includes step-by-step guides to creating delicious confections of high quality with the minimum of difficulty, and the book has been designed to create an unforgettable experience in the art of chocolate cookery. As you turn the pages, be prepared for a feast of delights to stimulate the taste buds and conjure up chocolate fantasies. The recipes include wonderfully indulgent yet quick-to-make desserts, rich sweets, luxurious gateaux and a wide range of cakes and biscuits for teatime treats, many of which do not require baking.

I feel sure that this new book will provide you with many happy hours in the kitchen and inspiration for every possible culinary occasion.

Mary Ford

The Origins of Chocolate

Food of the Gods

A Mexican Indian myth tells us that Quetzalcoatl, the Aztec god of the Wind and Fertility, presented cocoa to mankind. The Aztecs, in turn, called cocoa the 'Food of the Gods' and drank it in their sacred ceremonies. At the court of their emperor, Montezuma, a frothy chocolate confection made from cocoa beans was supped from gold goblets. Today, the cocoa tree is still officially known as Theobroma, literally meaning 'God Food'. It was named by the Swedish botanist, Linnaeus, who considered it to be an extraordinarily wholesome beverage, a divine drink.

Cocoa comes to the West

When Columbus sailed to South America in 1502, he was introduced to cocoa, which was then a bitter drink. However, it fell to a later explorer, Hernando Cortez, who conquered Mexico, to bring cocoa back to Europe. He imported beans from his own plantation in Mexico into Spain, where it was brewed into 'chocolat' with the addition of spices to improve the bitter flavour. Eventually sugar was added to make the brew more palatable. Spain held a monopoly on the cocoa bean trade for many years and, at that time, chocolate was a highly exclusive drink for the rich and influential Spanish Grandees.

A century later, a Spanish princess took her treasured cocoa beans to the French Court and chocolate quickly became a favourite drink in Europe, although it remained a luxury available only to the very wealthy. During the eighteenth century, chocolate became available to the clientele in the fashionable Coffee Houses and, by the end of that century, an innovative process involving grinding the beans with a steam engine was used by Dr Joseph Fry to produce cocoa powder. Chocolate was still exclusively drunk as a beverage during this time, however, and it was not until the end of the nineteenth century that a Swiss manufacturer, Daniel Peter, added condensed milk to cocoa to produce the solid milk chocolate known today.

The Bean

Chocolate is obtained from the fruit of the cocoa tree (Theobroma cacao) which grows to a height of 15m (48ft) but, when cultivated, is pruned to a height of 6m (19ft) to enable the fruit to be harvested with long poles. Five years of careful cultivation are required before trees produce fruit, so plantations can take quite a while before they become productive, and represent a considerable investment in time and money.

The cocoa fruits, shaped rather like a rugby ball about 20.5cm (8in) long, grow directly on the stem or thick branches of the tree, which flowers continuously throughout the year. Although the tree can produce as many as 10,000 pale pink, scentless blooms, only twenty to thirty blossoms will mature into fruit. Each fruit contains thirty to forty seeds in a gelatinous pulp. It is these seeds which are used to produce the highly prized chocolate.

The trees require very precise growing conditions: a light soil, moist climate, constant temperature between 20°C (68°F) and 35°C (95°F), and a particular combination of sunlight and shade at a maximum altitude of 605m (1969ft). These requirements are found only in latitudes within 20° of the Equator and the majority of the world crop is cultivated in Equatorial West Africa, Brazil, Equador, the Caribbean Islands and parts of Asia.

Making Chocolate

When the fruits are ripe, they are cut from the tree and chopped open. The seeds and pulp are then piled into special boxes and covered with leaves so that a process known as 'fermentation' can take place. As the temperature rises, the pulp is digested and the beans begin to develop their characteristic flavour. At this stage, however, they are extremely bitter and unsuitable for processing.

Following fermentation, the beans turn dark brown and the skin thins. The beans can then be dried outdoors, in the sun, before shipping to the processors in Europe. In the factory, the beans are carefully inspected to remove impurities before being roasted in enclosed cylinders to further develop the flavour.

After roasting, the beans are ground into a liquid paste which is then squeezed under high pressure to extract the cocoa butter and to separate the cocoa solids into cakes. The cakes are processed into cocoa powder, which is the main ingredient of chocolate. Legally, however, to be called chocolate, the fat content must be cocoa butter and the finished product is then known as couverture. Scotts 'Chocolat' is a high quality couverture specially made for home baking and desserts. When vegetable fat is used, the product is known as baker's chocolate, sold under trade names such as 'Scotbloc'.

How to Melt Scotbloc

The method shown is a quick and easy way to melt chocolate flavoured coatings such as Scotbloc.

A double-boiler saucepan should preferably be used as this prevents scorching, but alternatively a heat-proof bowl can be used over an ordinary saucepan which is small enough to support the bowl without it touching the base. The water level should not be allowed to touch the bowl.

Note: This method can also be used to melt 'Chocolat' in recipes which do not require tempering.

1 Working in a cool room temperature, place broken pieces into a heat-proof bowl.

2 Stand the bowl over a pan of simmering, not boiling, water and stir until the chocolate is almost melted.

3 Remove from the heat and continue stirring until chocolate is smooth and completely melted. Keep it warm, stirring occasionally, to prevent it from setting while in use.

Melting Scotbloc in a Microwave

To melt 225g (8oz) of plain Scotbloc in a microwave, place broken pieces, in a non-metallic bowl and microwave for 4-5 minutes on a medium setting, stirring once. Times are based on a 650W microwave oven. Individual ovens will vary, so check during heating. Milk chocolate will need slightly less time.

When just softened, remove from the microwave and stir well until the chocolate has completely melted. It is important not to overheat beyond the point where the chocolate is just soft, as this makes it grainy and unmanageable.

Couverture Chocolate

Couverture chocolate, such as Scotts Chocolat, is the purest form of chocolate and has an excellent flavour. It has a glossy appearance, making it ideal for high quality work where a smooth finish is required, and is less sweet than baker's chocolate. Couverture has a higher fat content and is highly recommended for all chocolate cookery although baker's chocolate, such as Scotbloc, can also be used for all the recipes in this book. Couverture is available from most supermarkets, confectioners or specialist shops. As blocks of dessert chocolate are usually made by a different process (and should be treated as baker's chocolate), care should be taken to ensure that the chocolate purchased is pure couverture. This is available in plain, milk and white varieties. Milk couverture has a lighter, sweeter flavour than plain, which is stronger and more bitter but is available in sweetened or unsweetened form. White couverture is produced from a combination of sugar and milk with cocoa butter.

Moisture adversely affects couverture, which should never be placed in a refrigerator. Tempering couverture is necessary when couverture is used for moulding or coating but not necessarily for cooking. Tempering creates a good gloss on a hard, brittle surface and removes the possibility of bloom developing. As milk and white couverture softens more quickly than plain, temperatures should be kept 1°C (2°F) lower during all stages of tempering.

Tempering Couverture (Chocolat)

Note: Do not use this method for Scotbloc or when incorporating Chocolat into mixtures. It is only necessary to temper Chocolat when stated in the recipes.

1 Break Chocolat into small pieces and place in heat-proof bowl.

2 Stand the bowl over a pan of simmering, not boiling, water and stir until the Chocolat is melted.

3 Heat and stir the Chocolat slowly until a temperature of 46°C (115°F) is reached. **Reduce all temperatures by 1°C (2°F) for milk Chocolat.**

4 Remove the bowl from the heat and stand it in cold water. Stir the Chocolat until it cools to 27-28°C (80-82°F).

5 Return the bowl to the saucepan until the temperature of the Chocolat reaches 31°C (88°F). Remove from the heat.

6 Test a small amount of Chocolat on greaseproof paper. If it does not set within 5 minutes, repeat steps 3-5. Keep the Chocolat at 31°C (88°F) whilst in use.

Baker's Chocolate

Baker's chocolate, such as Scotbloc, has almost all the cocoa butter content replaced with vegetable fat with the addition of sugar, milk powder and emulsifiers such as lecithin (made from soya beans). It is readily available in supermarkets as blocks in plain, milk or white varieties.

Scotbloc is extremely easy to use and can be placed in a refrigerator to set if necessary. Easily melted over a pan of hot water, Scotbloc should, however, be kept away from contact with steam or moisture as this will cause thickening.

White baker's chocolate does not always melt as well as dark. To ensure a really smooth texture, stand a second bowl in hot water and carefully pour the melted chocolate into this through a fine metal sieve.

Colouring White Scotbloc

A whole range of imaginative design possibilities are opened up by colouring white Scotbloc.

1 The Scotbloc should be melted over a pan of hot water (see p.10)

2 When melted, a small amount of edible powder or oil-based colouring should be added.

3 Thoroughly mix the colouring into the chocolate, using a wooden spoon.

Cocoa Powder

Manufactured from cocoa butter, and having a bitter taste, cocoa powder is the most economical chocolate flavouring for cakes and icing. A milder, sweeter taste is obtained from drinking chocolate, which contains sugar.

Chocolate Decorations

Chocolate can be used to add a decorative finishing touch to all cakes and desserts. Decorative shapes can easily be created from melted chocolate, as shown below, and, with the use of coloured white chocolate, do not have to be restricted to the basic brown 'chocolate' colour. Coloured chocolate is particularly appropriate for making the eye-catching decorations that appeal to children of all ages but the colour could be co-ordinated with the flavouring used or with ingredients such as oranges or cherries.

An extremely quick and effective decoration can be made from grated Scotbloc or Chocolat. The wrapped Scotbloc block should be placed in the refrigerator to chill or Chocolat left in a cool place, and then a coarse grater used to shave off pieces. Vermicelli can also be used as a topping, and can be combined with chocolate curls or shapes.

To save time, Scotts have created a range of ready-to-use numbers, letters, leaves, hearts and decorative shapes for use by busy cooks. The letters and numbers are especially helpful for the inexperienced cake decorator but, with a little ingenuity and imagination, all these products can create a truly individual confection such as the unusual carrot birthday cake on page 62 or the elegant dessert on page 72.

NOTE: If using Chocolat, it is necessary to temper the chocolate (see page 11). If using Scotbloc, melt in the usual way (see page 10).

Making cut-outs:
1 Spread the melted or tempered chocolate onto waxed paper and shake slightly to make an even surface. When nearly set, cut into shapes as required.

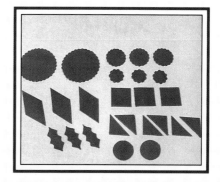

2 To ensure clean edges on each shape, press cutters firmly while cutting, without twisting. Leave to harden on greaseproof paper before using as decoration.

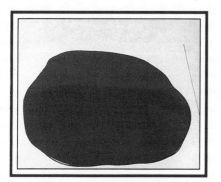

Making curls:
1 Pour melted or tempered chocolate onto a marble slab. Spread the chocolate thinly with a palette knife and leave until just set.

2 Holding a sharp knife at an angle of 45°, shave the surface of the chocolate to form curls. The thickness can be varied by altering the angle of the blade.

3 Place the curls on greaseproof paper and leave to set before using as decoration.

Hints and Tips

Storing
Chocolate should be stored in a cool dry place, preferably at 10°C (50°F). Do not store chocolate in the refrigerator.

As chocolate easily absorbs strong odours, opened blocks, buttons or grated chocolate should be sealed in waxed paper before storing.

Melting
Melt chocolate slowly on a very low heat, stirring gently.

Never try to hurry the melting process by turning up the heat.

Do not cover chocolate whilst being melted, or chocolate which is melted.

Buttons, or chocolate which has been grated or cut into small pieces, will melt more quickly and easily than block chocolate.

Melted chocolate should be stirred slowly when directed, not beaten, as this forms bubbles.

If melted chocolate is too thick, thin it with a small amount of lard - never add water as this causes chocolate to stiffen.

Coating
Scotbloc is better for coating cakes as it cuts more easily than couverture chocolate.

Couverture
Couverture has a superior taste and is thoroughly recommended for all confections in this book.

Couverture requires tempering where specified.

General
Keep chocolate away from direct sunlight as much as possible.

Work in a cool room 18°C (65°F) when using chocolate.

Do not allow water to come into contact with chocolate (unless specified in the recipe) and ensure that all utensils are absolutely dry.

When handling chocolate or sweets, wear disposable plastic gloves.

Grating

Before grating chocolate, place the wrapped chocolate block in the refrigerator for an hour to chill.

When grating chocolate, use a coarse grater.

Grated chocolate makes a quick and attractive topping for desserts and ice-cream and is a useful coating for cakes.

Grated chocolate can be used in place of vermicelli.

Chocolate Shavings

When making chocolate shavings, allow the block to reach 27°C (80°F) in a warm room and then finely 'shave' the chocolate with a potato peeler. Use long smooth strokes to achieve a quick curl.

Piping

Piping chocolate can be made by mixing a few drops of water with melted chocolate.

Keep piping chocolate warm, but not hot, whilst in use by standing basin over hot water.

Use small or medium sized piping bags for decorating chocolate confectionery.

Cocoa

Cocoa powder is the most economical chocolate flavouring for use in cooking.

Cocoa powder should be sieved with the dry ingredients where possible.

Colouring White Chocolate

White chocolate can be coloured using confectioner's dusting powder or special oil-based colouring. A very small amount of colour should be thoroughly worked into the melted chocolate until the desired colour is achieved.

Tempering

Always check whether the recipe requires tempering as it is not always necessary.

It is essential to use the temperatures specified for milk or plain couverture for correct results.

Couverture can also be cooled on a marble slab during the tempering process.

Coffee and Hazelnut Cups

Cups
70g (2½oz) plain Scotbloc

Decoration
toasted hazelnuts, chopped

Filling
70g (2½oz) plain Scotbloc or Chocolat
2 tablespoons readymade, strong coffee, cold
30g (1oz) butter
1 egg yolk, size 3

makes 10

1 **For the cups:** Melt the chocolate, then pour into double thickness paper cups. Pour out excess. Repeat three times. 10 cups required. Remove paper when set.

2 **For the filling:** Melt the chocolate with the coffee, in a bowl over hot water. Then beat in butter and egg yolk.

3 When almost set, pipe the mixture into the cups using a star piping tube. Decorate with toasted hazelnuts.

Honey and Bran Treats

115g (4oz) plain Scotbloc or Chocolat
60g (2oz) butter or margarine
2 tablespoons clear honey
85g (3oz) branflakes
30g (1oz) walnuts, chopped

makes 18

1 Break the chocolate into pieces. Gently heat the chocolate, butter and honey in a pan over low heat, stirring until melted.

2 Thoroughly mix in the branflakes and walnuts until covered.

3 Turn into a lined 18cm (7in) square cake tin. Smooth the surface and chill until set. Cut into squares.

Chocolate Tea-time Crunchies

Crunchies

200g (7oz) rich tea biscuits
2 tablespoons drinking chocolate or cocoa
30g (1oz) caster sugar
115g (4oz) margarine
1 large tablespoon golden syrup

Topping

60g (2oz) plain Scotbloc or Chocolat

**Note: If using Chocolat for the topping, it
must be tempered (see p.11).**

Decoration

white Scotbloc, grated

makes 25

1 Grease and line an 18cm (7in) square tin with greaseproof paper. Crush biscuits and place into a bowl with chocolate powder and sugar. Stir thoroughly.

2 Melt the margarine and syrup in a pan then mix it into the dry ingredients. Immediately spread evenly into the tin.

3 Melt the plain chocolate and spread over the top. Sprinkle white chocolate over the top before it sets. Leave to set. Cut into squares.

Marshmallow Crisps

Crisps

285g (10oz) milk Scotbloc or Chocolat

15 marshmallows

115g (4oz) rice crispies

**Note: If using Chocolat in this recipe
it must be tempered (see p.11).**

makes 15

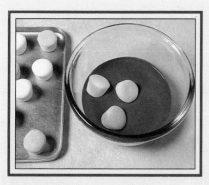

1 Melt the chocolate in a bowl over hot water. Drop a few marshmallows into the chocolate.

2 Carefully cover the marshmallows with the chocolate, using a fork. Then lift to remove excess chocolate and drop into the rice crispies.

3 Immediately roll to cover the chocolate. Leave in the bowl for two minutes before transferring onto a tray to set.

Chocolate Kirsch Logs

Log

115g (4oz) plain Scotbloc or Chocolat, grated
60g (2oz) blanched almonds, finely chopped
60g (2oz) icing sugar, sieved
1 tablespoon Kirsch
1 egg white, size 3

Coating

115g (4oz) plain Scotbloc or Chocolat, grated

Filling

30g (1oz) butter
1 tablespoon icing sugar, sieved
1 egg yolk
60g (2oz) glacé cherries, finely chopped

Decoration

glacé cherries

1 **For the log:** Mix the grated chocolate and almonds together. Then stir in the icing sugar and Kirsch.

2 Gradually mix in sufficient egg white to form a paste.

3 Spread the mixture on foil or silicone paper to cover an area 30.5 x 10cm (12 x 4in).

4 **For the filling:** Cream the butter and icing sugar together in a small bowl.

5 Then thoroughly beat in the egg yolk until light and fluffy.

6 Stir in the finely chopped cherries.

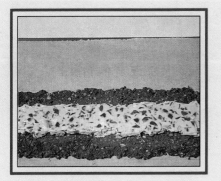

7 Spread the filling evenly along the centre, as shown.

8 Fold the sides over to enclose the filling, mould into a long roll.

9 **For the coating:** Immediately spread the grated chocolate onto greaseproof paper, then lightly roll the log over it to cover. Chill until required.

Ginger and Hazelnut Treats

Treats

225g (8oz) readymade marzipan

1 teaspoon honey

30g (1oz) glacé ginger, finely chopped

30g (1oz) hazelnuts, chopped and toasted

Dipping

115g (4oz) plain or milk Scotbloc or Chocolat

Note: If using Chocolat for dipping, it must be tempered (see p.11).

makes 16

1 Knead the marzipan until pliable. Add honey, ginger and hazelnuts and mix until evenly distributed.

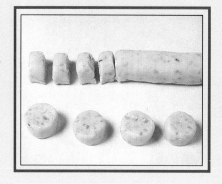

2 Dust work surface with icing sugar, then roll marzipan to 2cm (¾in) diameter. Cut marzipan into 1cm (½in) pieces and place on waxed paper to dry for 12 hours.

3 Melt chocolate over hot water. Using a fork, pick up a piece of marzipan and submerge to top edge. Lift out and drain. Place on waxed paper to set.

Chocolate Honey Toffee

Toffee
225g (8oz) clear honey
60g (2oz) soft brown sugar
115g (4oz) butter
2 teaspoons ground cinnamon

Coating
85g (3oz) white Scotbloc

makes 16

1 Grease a 20.5cm (8in) square tin with butter. Gently heat the honey and sugar in a heavy pan, stirring continuously until dissolved. Stir in butter until melted.

2 Boil mixture to small crack stage. Temperature will be 142°C (286°F) on the sugar thermometer. Remove from heat and beat in cinnamon.

3 Immediately pour into the tin. Mark into squares with a knife when almost set. When cold break up and dip into melted chocolate. Leave to set on waxed paper.

Liqueur Coconut Logs

Logs	Coating
225g (8oz) white Scotbloc	30g (1oz) desiccated coconut
150ml (¼ pint) condensed milk	
¼ teaspoon vanilla essence	makes 30
60g (2oz) desiccated coconut	
1 teaspoon liqueur or rum	

1 **For the logs:** Melt the chocolate, condensed milk and essence in a pan over a low heat.

2 Remove from heat, then stir in the coconut and liqueur or rum. Leave to cool and then shape into logs.

3 **For the coating:** Roll the logs on a tray covered in coconut. Chill until required.

Ginger Truffles

Truffles

60g (2oz) butter

60ml (2 fluid oz) double cream

1 teaspoon ground ginger

200g (7oz) milk Scotbloc or Chocolat

30g (1oz) glacé ginger, finely chopped

1 egg yolk, size 3

1 tablespoon Drambuie

Decoration

cocoa powder, sieved

crystallised ginger

makes 20

1 Combine the butter, cream and ground ginger in a saucepan. Cook on low heat until butter melts and cream bubbles around edge. Then remove from heat.

2 Chop the chocolate and add to the mixture. Cover with a lid until the chocolate melts. Stir until smooth.

3 Mix in the glacé ginger, egg yolk and Drambuie. Chill until firm. Form into balls and roll in cocoa powder to cover. Top with ginger.

Chocolate Marzipans

Marzipans
225g (8oz) readymade marzipan

Dipping
225g (8oz) milk or plain Scotbloc or Chocolat

Note: If using Chocolat for dipping this must be tempered (see p.11).

Decoration
hazelnuts
walnuts, halved
roasted almonds, chopped

makes 24

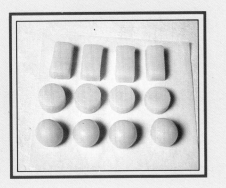

1 Roll out and cut the marzipan into squares and rounds, using icing sugar for dusting. Form balls from the cuttings. Leave to dry for 12 hours on waxed paper.

2 Melt the chocolate in a bowl over low heat. Using a fork, dip each marzipan piece, drain slightly then place onto waxed paper.

3 Before the chocolate sets, top or roll the sweets with nuts of choice. Leave to set.

Coconut Surprise

Base

85g (3oz) desiccated coconut

60g (2oz) glacé cherries, chopped

30g (1oz) seedless raisins

grated rind of ½ orange

2 eggs, size 3, beaten;

Decoration

200g (7oz) white Scotbloc

makes 24

1 Grease and base line a 28 x 18cm (11 x 7in) baking tin. Mix together the coconut, cherries, raisins, orange rind and beaten eggs.

2 Spread mixture evenly in the baking tray. Bake at 180°C (350°F) or gas mark 4 for approximately 10 minutes, or golden brown. Leave to cool in tin.

3 Turn over onto a tray. Cover with melted chocolate, using a serrated scraper for design. Allow to set and cut into shapes.

Marshmallow Nut Fudge

Fudge
285g (10oz) marshmallows
85g (3oz) butter, cubed
1 tablespoon water
170g (6oz) plain Scotbloc or Chocolat
few drops vanilla essence
170g (6oz) walnuts, coarsely chopped

makes 40

1 Melt the marshmallows, butter and water in a pan over low heat, stirring occasionally.

2 Chop the chocolate, and add with the essence and walnuts to the mixture. Stir until evenly mixed and the chocolate has melted.

3 Line the base of a 23 x 10cm (9 x 4in) loaf tin with foil. Pour mixture into tin. When cool, refrigerate wrapped in foil before cutting into cubes.

Ginger Thins

Sweets

85g (3oz) plain Scotbloc

2 pieces stem ginger, well drained

Decoration

30g (1oz) white Scotbloc

makes 15

1 Melt the chocolate in a bowl over a pan of hot water. Coarsely chop the well-drained ginger and stir into the melted chocolate.

2 Carefully spoon the mixture into paper sweet cases. Leave in a cool place until set.

3 Remove from the paper cases then pipe melted white chocolate over the surface, as shown.

No-Cook Crunch

Crunch
225g (8oz) digestive biscuits
60g (2oz) raisins
60g (2oz) glacé cherries, chopped
2 tablespoons golden syrup
115g (4oz) butter
115g (4oz) milk Scotbloc or Chocolat

Topping
115g (4oz) milk Scotbloc or Chocolat
60g (2oz) butter
170g (6oz) icing sugar, sieved

Decoration
glacé cherries
walnuts

1 **For the crunch**: Break up the biscuits into crumbs. Add the raisins and chopped cherries.

2 Melt the syrup and butter together, then mix into the dry ingredients.

3 Melt the chocolate and thoroughly stir into the mixture.

4 Press the mixture into a 20.5cm (8in) flan ring or loose bottom tin. Chill in a refrigerator for at least 1 hour.

5 **For the topping:** Melt the chocolate and butter together in a pan over low heat.

6 Stir in the icing sugar until a paste is formed.

7 Remove from heat and spread the topping over the crunch.

8 Immediately mark the top with a fork to form the pattern shown.

9 **For the decoration:** Lightly press half cherries and walnuts onto the cake-top as shown.

Coconut Chocolate Clusters

115g (4oz) plain Scotbloc or Chocolat

115g (4oz) milk Scotbloc or Chocolat

115g (4oz) desiccated coconut, toasted

2 teaspoons instant coffee granules

30g (1oz) butter, melted

makes 40

may be stored up to one month

1 Melt the plain and milk chocolate in a bowl set over a pan of hot water.

2 Thoroughly stir in the coconut, coffee granules and the melted butter.

3 Immediately spoon out on to non-stick baking paper. Leave in a cool place until set.

Chocolate and Hazelnut Slice

Slice
255g (9oz) plain Scotbloc or Chocolat
170g (6oz) evaporated milk
285g (10oz) digestive biscuits, crushed
115g (4oz) roasted hazelnuts, ground

Decoration
60g (2oz) plain Scotbloc or Chocolat, melted
30g (1oz) white Scotbloc, melted

Note: If using Chocolat for decoration, it must be tempered (see p.11).

makes 15

  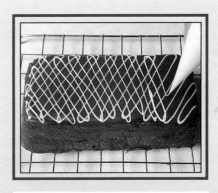

1 **For the slice:** Gently heat chocolate and evaporated milk until melted. Place crushed biscuits and hazelnuts into a bowl. Stir in the chocolate mixture.

2 Spoon the mixture into a lined and greased 455g (1lb) loaf tin. Smooth top with a palette knife. Leave in refrigerator for 12 hours. Turn the cake out onto a tray.

3 **For the decoration:** Spread the melted plain chocolate over the top. Then pipe the white chocolate, as shown. Cut into slices.

Peppermint Diamonds

Biscuit Base
2 level teaspoons cocoa powder

115g (4oz) self-raising flour, sieved

60g (2oz) crushed cornflakes

85g (3oz) soft brown sugar

115g (4oz) margarine

Filling
225g (8oz) icing sugar, sieved

2 tablespoons water

¼ teaspoon peppermint essence

green colouring, optional

makes 26

Topping
145g (5oz) plain Scotbloc or Chocolat

30g (1oz) white Scotbloc

Note: If using Chocolat for the topping, it must be tempered (see p.11).

1 **For the base:** Place all dry ingredients into a bowl. Melt and stir in the margarine.

2 Press the mixture into a swiss roll tin 28 x 20.5cm (11 x 8in).

3 Bake at 180°C (350°F) or gas mark 4 for approximately 20 minutes. Remove from tin and leave to cool on greaseproof paper.

4 **For the filling:** Blend the icing sugar, water, essence and colouring together to form soft icing.

5 Spread the filling evenly over the baked base. Leave to set for one hour.

6 **For the topping:** Melt the plain and white Scotbloc in separate bowls. Spread the plain chocolate carefully over the icing.

7 Using the white chocolate, immediately pipe lines over the top, as shown.

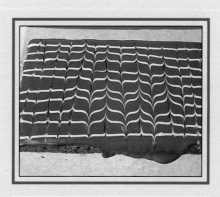

8 Very quickly draw a cocktail stick across the lines to form the pattern shown. Leave to set for one hour.

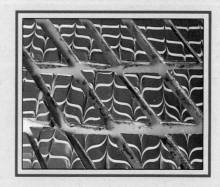

9 When set, cut into diamonds using a sharp, serrated knife.

Muesli Bars

Bars

145g (5oz) plain Scotbloc or Chocolat
3 tablespoons golden syrup
30g (1oz) butter
225g (8oz) muesli

Topping

145g (5oz) milk Scotbloc or Chocolat

Note: If using Chocolat for the topping it must be tempered (see p.11).

makes 18

1 **For the base:** Gently heat the chocolate, golden syrup and butter in a pan over low heat, until melted. Then stir in the muesli.

2 Line the base of a shallow 18cm (7in) square tin with non-stick baking paper. Press the mixture evenly into the tin.

3 **For the topping:** Melt the chocolate and spread over the surface. When almost set, mark with a fork then chill until set. Cut into bars.

Coconut and Fruit Fingers

Fingers

285g (10oz) white Scotbloc
60g (2oz) raisins
60g (2oz) sultanas
60g (2oz) dried (no need to soak) apricots,
chopped
30g (1oz) toasted oat cereal

Decoration

30g (1oz) shredded coconut, toasted

makes 12

1 Grease an 18cm (7in) square cake
tin with butter.

2 Melt the chocolate in a bowl over
a pan of hot water. Remove pan
from heat and fold in the fruit and
cereal.

3 Transfer mixture to prepared tin
and smooth the surface. Sprinkle
with toasted coconut and chill until
set. Cut into bars.

Caramel Shortcake

Shortcake

115g (4oz) softened butter

1 egg yolk, size 3

1 tablespoon water

200g (7oz) plain flour, sieved

1 teaspoon baking powder

Filling

400g (14oz) condensed milk

60g (2oz) butter

2 tablespoons golden syrup

1 teaspoon vanilla essence

Topping

85g (3oz) plain Scotbloc or Chocolat

85g (3oz) milk Scotbloc or Chocolat

Note: If using Chocolat for topping, it must be tempered (see p.11).

makes 21

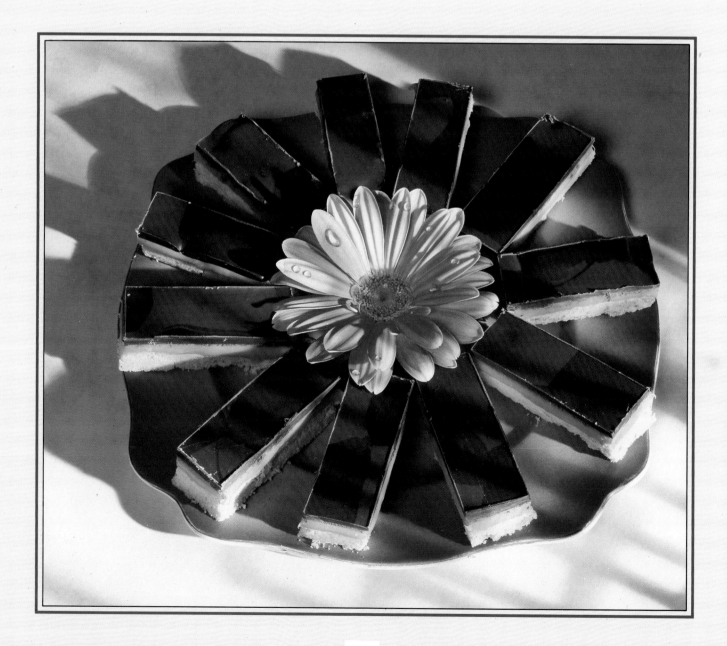

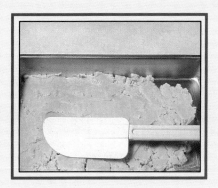

1 **For the shortcake:** Grease a 28 x 18cm (11 x 7in) shallow baking tin. Beat together butter, egg yolk and water until creamy.

2 Sieve the flour and baking powder together, then mix into the mixture to form a dough.

3 Press the dough into the prepared tin to form an even layer.

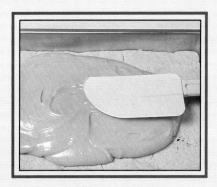

4 Bake at 180°C (350°F) or Gas Mark 4 for 20 minutes or until golden brown, then leave to cool in the tin.

5 **For the filling:** Gently heat the condensed milk, butter, syrup and essence in a pan until melted. Then boil for 5 minutes, stirring occasionally.

6 Cool slightly and spread the mixture over the shortcake in the tin. Leave to set.

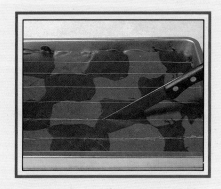

7 **For the topping:** Melt the chocolate in separate bowls over a pan of hot water.

8 Using a spoon, drop alternate milk and plain chocolate onto the filling to form the pattern shown.

9 Leave to set, then cut into fingers before removing from the tin.

Chocolate Rock Cookies

Cookies

170g (6oz) soft margarine

285g (10oz) caster sugar

1 large egg

285g (10oz) plain flour, sieved

60g (2oz) cocoa powder

85g (3oz) milk Scotbloc or Chocolat, chopped

approximately 3 tablespoons milk

Decoration

icing sugar, sieved

makes 30

1 Cream the margarine and sugar until light and fluffy. Gradually beat in the egg.

2 Fold in the flour, cocoa powder and finely chopped chocolate. Add sufficient milk to form a dough-like consistency.

3 Spoon mixture well apart on a lightly greased baking tray. Flatten slightly. Bake at 190°C (375°F) or gas mark 5 for 10-12 minutes. Dust with icing sugar when cold.

Coconut Munchies

225g (8oz) milk Scotbloc or Chocolat

1 egg, size 3

115g (4oz) caster sugar

115g (4oz) desiccated coconut

115g (4oz) glacé cherries, halved

Note: If using Chocolat in this recipe, it must be tempered (see p.11).

makes 40

1 Grease a 28 x 18cm (11 x 7in) shallow tin with butter. Melt the chocolate and pour it into the tin. Leave to set.

2 Beat the egg and sugar together, then add the coconut and cherries.

3 Spread the mixture over the chocolate. Bake at 180°C (350°F) or gas mark 4, for approximately 20 minutes until light and golden brown. Cut when cold.

Chocolate Finger Biscuits

Biscuits

115g (4oz) butter

115g (4oz) caster sugar

2 egg yolks, size 3

1 teaspoon vanilla essence

170g (6oz) plain flour, sieved

60g (2oz) plain Scotbloc or Chocolat

Decoration

115g (4oz) plain Scotbloc or Chocolat

60g (2oz) desiccated coconut, toasted

Note: If using Chocolat for the decoration, it must be tempered (see p.11).

makes 32

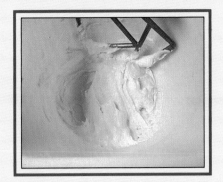

1 **For the biscuits:** Cream the butter and sugar until light and fluffy.

2 Thoroughly beat in the egg yolks and vanilla essence.

3 Carefully fold in the flour until free from lumps. Do not over mix.

4 Melt and stir in the 60g (2oz) of chocolate.

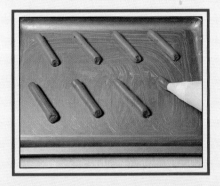

5 Using a 1.5cm (⅝in) plain piping tube, pipe finger lengths - 7.5cm (3in) - onto greased baking sheets.

6 Bake at 190°C (350°F) or gas mark 5 for approximately 10 minutes or until golden brown. Leave to cool on the baking sheets for 5 minutes.

7 Carefully remove the biscuits from the trays and transfer to a cooling wire. Leave until cold.

8 **For the decoration:** Melt the 115g (4oz) of chocolate in a bowl and dip each end of the biscuits, as shown. Place onto waxed paper.

9 Before the chocolate sets, sprinkle with toasted coconut.

Chocolate Empire Biscuits

Biscuits

145 (5oz) butter or margarine

60g (2oz) caster sugar

225g (8oz) plain flour, sieved

Filling

Scotts Raspberry Conserve

Dipping

170g (6oz) milk or plain Scotbloc or Chocolat

Note: If using Chocolat for dipping, it must be tempered (see p.11).

Decoration

Scotts Real Chocolate Hearts

makes 12

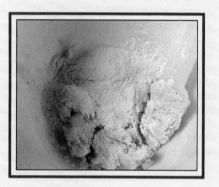

1 Cream the butter, or margarine, and sugar together in a mixer. Carefully fold in the flour until bound.

2 Roll out on floured surface and cut 24 biscuits 6.5cm (2½in) diameter. Bake on greased tray at 180°C (350°F) or gas mark 4 for 30 minutes or until golden brown.

3 Cool on wire tray. Sandwich in pairs, using conserve for filling. Roll edge into shallow tray of melted chocolate and finish with heart shapes, as shown.

Chocolate Viennese Whirls

Whirls

225g (8oz) butter, softened

60g (2oz) icing sugar, sieved

½ teaspoon vanilla essence

225g (8oz) plain flour, sieved

30g (1oz) drinking chocolate

60g (2oz) cornflour

Dipping

115g (4oz) milk Scotbloc or Chocolat

Note: If using Chocolat for dipping, this must be tempered (see p.11).

makes 24

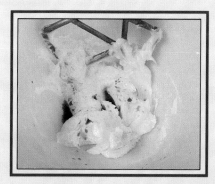

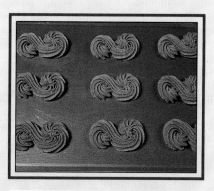

1 Cream the butter and sugar until light and fluffy. Add the essence and beat well.

2 Mix in flour, drinking chocolate and cornflour. Fill piping bag fitted with 1.5cm (⅝in) star nozzle and pipe 'S' shapes onto greased baking sheets.

3 Bake at 180ºC (350ºF) or gas mark 4 for approximately 25 minutes until golden brown. When cold dip into melted chocolate. Leave to set on greaseproof paper.

Chocolate Wheatmeal Biscuits

Biscuits
285g (10oz) wholemeal flour
½ teaspoon salt
1 teaspoon baking powder
60g (2oz) soft brown sugar
170g (6oz) butter
2 eggs, size 3, lightly beaten

Dipping
115g (4oz) milk or plain Scotbloc
or Chocolat

**Note: If using Chocolat for dipping,
this must be tempered (see p.11).**

Decoration
Scotts Real Chocolate Leaves

makes 24

1 Dust two baking trays with flour. Place the wholemeal flour, salt, baking powder and sugar in a bowl. Rub in the butter.

2 Using a fork, stir in the beaten eggs, then knead to a stiff dough. On a floured work surface, roll out the dough to 5mm (¼in) thick. Cut out 5cm (2in) rounds.

3 Place onto the baking sheets. Bake at 180°C (350°F) or gas mark 4 for 15-20 minutes. Cool and then dip the bases into melted chocolate and decorate.

Chocolate Chip Cakes

60g (2oz) plain Scotbloc or Chocolat

60g (2oz) soft tub margarine

60g (2oz) caster sugar

85g (3oz) self-raising flour

pinch salt

1 large egg

makes 12

1 Grate the chocolate. Place all the ingredients into a bowl.

2 Beat well with a wooden spoon for 2-3 minutes, until fully blended.

3 Spoon the mixture into twelve paper cases. Bake at 190°C (375°F) or gas mark 5 for approximately 20 minutes.

Chocolate Chip Rockies

60g (2oz) butter
60g (2oz) soft brown sugar
1 small egg, beaten
¼ teaspoon vanilla essence
grated rind of 1 orange
60g (2oz) plain flour
pinch of salt
85g (3oz) rolled oats
30g (1oz) plain Scotbloc or Chocolat, grated

Decoration
60g (2oz) plain Scotbloc or Chocolat, grated

makes 18

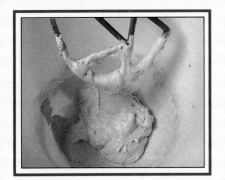 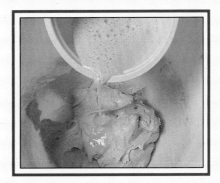 

1 Beat the butter and sugar until light and creamy.

2 Beat in the beaten egg and vanilla essence.

3 Thoroughly mix in the grated orange rind.

4 Sieve the flour and salt together then stir into the mixture with the rolled oats.

5 Lightly fold in the grated chocolate until evenly mixed.

6 Using a teaspoon, place spoonfuls on baking sheets lined with non-stick paper, approximately 10cm (4in) apart.

7 Bake in the oven at 180°C (350°F) or gas mark 4 for approximately 15 minutes.

8 When cooked, leave on tray for 5 minutes then place onto cooling wire.

9 While still warm sprinkle grated chocolate over each rock cake, as shown.

Mountain Sponge Cakes

Cakes

115g (4oz) self-raising flour
1 teaspoon baking powder
115g (4oz) caster sugar
115g (4oz) soft margarine
2 eggs, size 3
1 teaspoon vanilla essence

Coating

2 tablespoons apricot jam
1 tablespoon water
85g (3oz) plain Scotbloc or Chocolat,
grated

Decoration

white Scotbloc, melted
coloured Scotbloc, melted
Scotts Real Chocolate Hearts

makes 12

1 Sieve flour and baking powder together. Add sugar, margarine, eggs and vanilla essence. Beat until a soft dropping consistency is formed.

2 Divide mixture between paper cases and greased, base- lined dariole moulds. Bake at 190°C (375°F) gas mark 5 for 10-15 minutes until golden brown. Leave to cool.

3 Remove from moulds and trim tops if necessary. Heat jam and water and brush tops and sides with the glaze. Roll in grated chocolate. Decorate as shown.

Chocolate Surprise Cones

Cones

10 round ice cream cones

Filling

60g (2oz) unsalted chopped nuts, toasted
10 pink and white marshmallows
icing sugar, for tossing
200g (7oz) milk Scotbloc or Chocolat
4 tablespoons milk or evaporated milk, warmed

Decoration

vermicelli
hundreds and thousands
chopped nuts

makes 10

1 Stand the cones in a wire tray. Sprinkle some nuts in base. Chop marshmallows and toss in icing sugar. Mix with remaining nuts.

2 Melt chocolate in a basin over hot water. Beat in the warmed milk a little at a time. Leave until cool but soft (approximately 30 minutes).

3 Stir the marshmallows and nuts into the chocolate mixture and leave for 1 hour, until cold but sticky. Fill cones with mixture and dip top into decorations.

Marbled Sponge Slices

Base

170g (6oz) butter or margarine

170g (6oz) caster sugar

3 eggs, size 3, beaten

170g (6oz) self-raising flour

few drops pink food colouring

1 tablespoon cocoa powder

2 tablespoons boiling water

Topping (Fudge Icing)

60g (2oz) plain Scotbloc or Chocolat

60g (2oz) butter

225g (8oz) icing sugar, sieved

2 tablespoons milk

makes 24

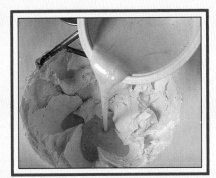

1 For the base: Grease a 28 x 18cm (11 x 7in) tin. Beat butter, or margarine, with the sugar until light and fluffy. Beat in eggs a little at a time.

2 Lightly fold the flour into the mixture until smooth.

3 Divide the mixture evenly between two bowls. Colour one half pink.

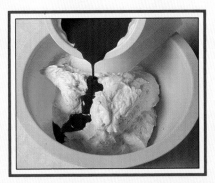

4 Blend the cocoa powder to a paste with the water and mix into the other half.

5 Spoon alternate mixtures into the tin. Swirl together using a wooden skewer. Bake at 180°C (350°F) or gas mark 4 for 25 to 30 minutes until golden. Leave to cool.

6 For the topping: Place all the topping ingredients into a bowl over hot water.

7 Stir until smooth and glossy. Then cool until thick enough for spreading.

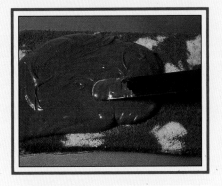

8 Upturn the cold base and spread the fudge over the top.

9 Moving the palette knife in a zig zag motion, pattern the top as shown. Leave to set and cut into bars.

Highland Tartlets

Pastry
225g (8oz) plain flour
145g (5oz) butter or margarine
2 tablespoons caster sugar
4 teaspoons cold water

Filling
Scotts Apple Jelly
60g (2oz) milk or plain Scotbloc or
Chocolat
2 eggs, size 3, separated

Decoration
whipped cream
chocolate cut-outs

makes 12

1 **For the pastry:** Sieve the flour into a bowl. Rub the butter or margarine into the flour until mixture resembles breadcrumbs.

2 Dissolve the sugar in the water. Make a well in the centre of the flour and then mix in the sugar solution, to form pastry.

3 Roll out to 3.5mm (⅛in) thick on a flour dusted board. Cut into circles to line patty tins. Prick well.

4 Bake at 180°C (350°F) or gas mark 4 for 12 to 15 minutes, until golden brown. Leave to cool on a wire tray.

5 **For the filling:** When cold, pipe Scotts apple jelly into the base of each tart.

6 Melt the chocolate in a bowl over hot water. Remove from heat and beat in the egg yolks a little at a time.

7 Whisk the egg whites, then carefully fold into the mixture.

8 Fill each tartlet with the mixture, using a small spoon. Leave until set.

9 Pipe fresh cream on top and decorate with chocolate cut-outs, as shown.

Lemon and Chocolate Layer Cake

Cake

225g (8oz) plain flour

pinch of salt

2 level teaspoons of baking powder

85g (3oz) margarine

85g (3oz) caster sugar

1 egg, size 3

2 teaspoons grated lemon rind

150ml (¼ pint) milk

115g (4oz) plain Scotbloc or Chocolat, coarsely grated

Decoration

icing sugar, sieved

1 Grease a 15cm (6in) cake tin and line the base with greased greaseproof paper. Sieve together flour, salt and baking powder. Rub in the margarine.

2 Add the sugar, egg, lemon rind and milk.

3 Stir the mixture with a wooden spoon until a soft dropping consistency is reached.

4 Spoon one third of the mixture into the tin, then sprinkle on some of the grated chocolate, as shown.

5 Spoon half the remaining mixture on top, then add more grated chocolate.

6 Spoon remaining mixture on top then, finally, sprinkle on the remaining grated chocolate.

7 Bake in oven at 190°C (375°F) or gas mark 5 for 15 minutes, then reduce heat to 180°C (350°F) or gas mark 4 for one hour.

8 When baked leave in tin for 30 minutes. Then remove from tin and leave to cool on a wire tray.

9 Using a fine sieve, dust the top with icing sugar.

Italian Chocolate Cake

Sponge
2 eggs, size 3
70g (2½oz) caster sugar
60g (2oz) plain flour, sieved

Filling
200g (7oz) low fat cheese
30g (1oz) caster sugar
145g (5oz) mixed crystallised fruits, chopped
30g (1oz) plain Scotbloc or Chocolat, grated rind of 1 orange or lemon, grated
2 tablespoons fruit flavoured liqueur

Topping
115g (4oz) milk or plain Scotbloc or Chocolat
60g (2oz) unsalted butter
1 egg, size 3
170g (6oz) icing sugar, sieved

Decoration
glacé fruits

58

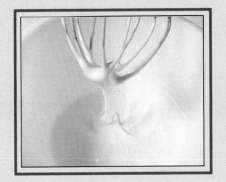

1 **For the sponge:** Grease an 18cm (7in) round tin and line base with greased greaseproof paper. Whisk eggs and caster sugar until light and fluffy.

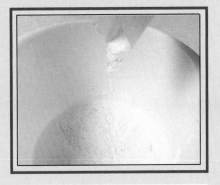

2 Carefully fold in the flour. Pour into tin and bake at 180°C (350°F) or Gas Mark 4 for 25-30 minutes or until golden brown.

3 Leave in the tin for 5 minutes then remove and cool on a wire tray. Remove greaseproof paper when cold.

4 **For the filling:** Cream the cheese and sugar. Add the fruits, chocolate and grated rind. Mix well to form a paste.

5 Cut the sponge into three layers. Sprinkle each layer with liqueur then spread filling over the bottom layer.

6 Place a layer on top then more filling. Place last layer on top and leave in a refrigerator to chill for 1 hour.

7 **For the topping:** Melt the chocolate and butter in a pan over hot water, stirring occasionally.

8 Thoroughly beat the egg and stir into the chocolate.

9 Remove from the heat and stir in the icing sugar. Then beat well. Leave to cool slightly until the mixture thickens. Spread over the cake and decorate.

Sachertorte

Torte
145g (5oz) butter
145g (5oz) caster sugar
2 eggs, size 3, separated
170g (6oz) plain Scotbloc or Chocolat, melted
115g (4oz) plain flour
½ teaspoon baking powder
¼ teaspoon almond essence

Filling
1 tablespoon rum
5 tablespoons apricot jam, sieved

Topping
115g (4oz) caster sugar
145g (5oz) water
145g (5oz) plain Scotbloc or Chocolat, melted
3 tablespoons warm water

Decoration
60g (2oz) milk Scotbloc or Chocolat, melted

1 Grease and flour a 23cm (9in) cake tin. **For the torte:** Beat the butter and sugar together until light and fluffy.

2 Thoroughly beat in the egg yolks, a little at a time.

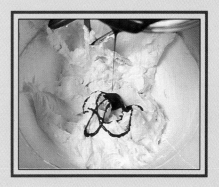

3 Beat in the melted chocolate until well blended.

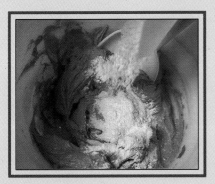

4 Sieve the flour, cornflour and baking powder together, then fold into the mixture.

5 Whisk the egg whites until stiff, fold into the mixture with the essence.

6 Transfer the mixture to the tin and bake at 150°C (300°F) or gas mark 2, for approximately 45 minutes or until baked.

7 **For the filling:** When the torte is cold cut into two. Brush on the rum then spread the purée over the bottom half and sandwich together.

8 **For topping:** Melt sugar in water over low heat. Do not stir. Boil to 115°C (240°F). Remove from heat. Stir the warm water into the chocolate. Mix into the hot syrup.

9 Leave the topping to cool, whisking occasionally until it thickens. Pour over the torte and leave to set. To decorate pipe SACHER across the top with milk chocolate.

Carrot Cake

Cake

3 eggs, size 3
340g (12oz) soft brown sugar
170ml (6 fluid oz) sunflower oil
2 teaspoon vanilla essence
60ml (2 fluid oz) soured cream
255g (9oz) plain wholemeal flour

1 teaspoon grated nutmeg
½ teaspoon salt
1 teaspoon bicarbonate of soda
315g (11oz) desiccated coconut
340g (12oz) carrots, grated

Topping

115g (4oz) full fat soft cheese
60g (2oz) butter
340g (12oz) icing sugar, sieved
juice of ½ lemon

Decoration

Scotts Real Chocolate Alphabet
Scotts Real Chocolate Leaves

1 **For the cake:** Line base and sides of a 20.5cm (8in) cake tin with greased greaseproof paper. Mix together eggs, sugar, oil, essence and soured cream.

2 Mix together flour, nutmeg, salt and bicarbonate of soda and then carefully fold into the mixture.

3 Add the coconut and mix thoroughly.

4 Add the grated carrot and mix thoroughly.

5 Transfer to the prepared cake tin and bake in the centre of the oven at 150°C (300°F) gas mark 2, for 1½ to 2 hours until well risen and firm to touch.

6 Allow to stand in the tin for 5 minutes then turn out onto a wire tray until cold.

7 **For the topping:** Mix together all the ingredients until smooth.

8 Spread on top of the cake and mark with a fork or serrated scraper, as shown.

9 Decorate the cake as appropriate.

Chocolate Birthday Sponge Cake

Sponge
225g (8oz) plain Scotbloc or Chocolat
225g (8oz) butter
225g (8oz) caster sugar
170g (6oz) plain flour, sieved
6 large eggs, separated

Filling
liqueur of choice
85g (3oz) Scotts Raspberry Conserve

Coating
60g (2oz) apricot jam, sieved
170g (6oz) almond paste
340g (12oz) white Scotbloc
pink powder food colouring

Decoration
Scotts Real Chocolate Hearts
Scotts Real Chocolate Alphabet

1 **For the sponge:** Melt the chocolate in a pan over hot water. Cream the butter and sugar in a bowl then quickly beat in the melted chocolate until evenly mixed.

2 Beat in the flour a little at a time, alternating with the egg yolks, until all is used.

3 Whisk the egg whites to a peak, then lightly fold into the mixture.

4 Spread the mixture evenly into a greased 20.5cm (8in) tin. Bake at 180°C (350°F) or gas mark 4 for approximately 45 minutes.

5 When baked cool on a wire tray. When cold cut into three layers. **For the filling:** Sprinkle with liqueur and fill with the conserve.

6 **For the coating:** Boil the apricot purée and brush over the top and sides. Cover with rolled out almond paste. Then brush the almond paste with more boiling apricot purée.

7 Melt the chocolate over a pan of hot water and mix in the powder colouring. Pour the chocolate over the almond paste. Leave to set.

8 **For the decoration:** Fix a ribbon around the base, then fix hearts as shown.

9 Using the alphabet letters fix message of choice to the cake-top.

Caribbean Cake

Cake

1 packet chocolate victoria sponge mix
60g (2oz) unsweetened desiccated coconut
1 tablespoon water, warm

Filling

60g (2oz) dried apricots, finely chopped
4 tablespoons dark rum
115g (4oz) plain Scotbloc or Chocolat
14g (½oz) butter
30g (1oz) unsweetened desiccated coconut
1 tablespoon instant coffee powder
1 tablespoon soft brown sugar
4 tablespoons water, boiling
4 tablespoons apricot jam

Decoration

300ml (½ pint) double cream, whipped
Scotts Real Chocolate Logs
Scotts Real Chocolate Leaves
jelly diamonds

1 **For the cake:** Grease and flour two 18cm (7in) square baking tins. Make up the sponge mix as instructed on the packet. Stir in the coconut and water.

2 Divide the mixture between the prepared tins and bake at 180°C (350°F) gas mark 4 for 20 to 30 minutes. Leave to cool on a wire tray.

3 Cut one cake in half horizontally. Crumb the other cake into a bowl.

4 **For the filling:** Soak the apricots in the rum for at least four hours.

5 Melt the chocolate and butter in a basin over hot water, stirring occasionally. Stir the coconut into the chocolate mixture.

6 In a separate bowl, blend the coffee, sugar and boiling water.

7 Spoon one-third of the cake crumbs into each of the apricot and rum, chocolate and coffee mixtures.

8 Spread one cut layer of cake with half the jam and place on a serving plate, jam side up. Spread the other half with jam and reserve.

9 Spread apricot mixture, chocolate, then coffee on base. Place second half on top, jam side down. Chill overnight then decorate as shown.

Orange and Chocolate Cake

340g (12oz) plain Scotbloc or Chocolat
115g (4oz) butter
85g (3oz) golden syrup
grated rind of 1 orange
115g (4oz) sultanas
340g (12oz) digestive biscuits, crushed
3 tablespoons dark rum

makes 24

1 Grease a 20.5cm (8in) round loose bottom sponge tin. Melt chocolate, butter and syrup over gentle heat, stirring until smooth and glossy for 5 minutes.

2 Stir in the orange rind, sultanas, crushed biscuits and rum.

3 Remove from heat and transfer the mixture into the cake tin. Leave to cool then chill until form. Remove from tin and cut into small wedges.

Peppermint Crunch Flan

Base

200g (7oz) digestive biscuits, crushed
60g (2oz) butter or margarine, melted
115g (4oz) plain Scotbloc or Chocolat, grated

Filling

3 egg yolks, size 3
85g (3oz) caster sugar
2 tablespoons creme de menthe
few drops green colouring
2 teaspoons powdered gelatine
2 tablespoons water
145g (5oz) double cream, whipped

Decoration

double cream, whipped
chocolate cut-outs
white Scotbloc, grated

1 For the base: Mix the biscuits with the melted butter. Stir in the grated chocolate. Press mixture into a lined 20.5cm (8in) loose bottom fluted flan tin. Chill.

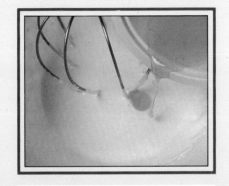

2 For the filling: Whisk egg yolks, then whisk in the sugar, flavour and colour until mixture thickens. Dissolve gelatine in the water, whisk into mixture.

3 Fold in the whipped cream. Pour mixture into flan case. Chill until firm. Decorate as shown.

Saucy Sponge Pudding

Sponge	Sauce
115g (4oz) butter	60g (2oz) plain Scotbloc or Chocolat
115g (4oz) caster sugar	300ml (½ pint) milk, hot
2 eggs, size 3, beaten	
115g (4oz) self-raising flour	Serves 4-6
30g (1oz) plain Scotbloc or Chocolat	

1 **For the sponge:** Cream butter and caster sugar together until light and fluffy. Beat in eggs and flour.

2 Coarsely grate the chocolate and fold into the mixture gently. Place mixture in a 1.1 litre (2 pint) ovenproof pudding basin.

3 **For the sauce:** Melt the chocolate in the hot milk and pour over the sponge. Bake at 170°C (325°F) gas mark 3 for approximately 50 minutes. Dust with icing sugar and serve.

Sugared Chocolate Pancakes

Pancakes
60g (2oz) plain flour
pinch of salt
2 tablespoons caster sugar
1 tablespoon oil
2 eggs, size 3, separated
6 tablespoons milk

Frying
2 tablespoons oil

Filling and Decoration
60g (2oz) plain Scotbloc or Chocolat, grated
caster sugar

makes 8

1 Sieve the flour, salt and sugar together into a bowl. Mix the oil, egg yolks and milk together then beat into the flour mixture to form a smooth batter.

2 Whisk the egg whites to form peaks, then fold into the batter.

3 Fry in lightly oiled pan. Cook one side, then sprinkle on chocolate and roll up. Place in well buttered dish, sprinkle with sugar and grill for 5-10 minutes. Serve.

Chocolate and Almond Slice

Slice

9 sponge fingers

115g (4oz) butter

60g (2oz) caster sugar

60g (2oz) ground almonds

60g (2oz) nibbed almonds

60g (2oz) plain cake crumbs

115g (4oz) plain Scotbloc or Chocolat

1 tablespoon rum (optional)

1 small can evaporated milk

Decoration

145ml (5 fluid oz) double or whipping cream

Scotts Real Chocolate Leaves

Serves 4-6

1 **For the slice:** Trim sides and ends of the sponge fingers.

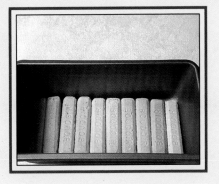

2 Place the sponge fingers in the bottom of a 910g (2lb) loaf tin.

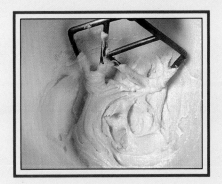

3 Cream together the butter and sugar until light and fluffy.

4 Thoroughly stir in the ground almonds, nibbed almonds and cake crumbs.

5 Melt the chocolate in a bowl over hot water. Stir the melted chocolate and then the rum into the crumb mixture.

6 Lightly whisk the evaporated milk and fold into the mixture.

7 Transfer the mixture to the loaf tin, spread evenly. Leave to set in a refrigerator for 12 hours.

8 Carefully remove from the tin and place onto a serving tray.

9 **For the decoration:** Pipe shells and rosettes, using the whipped cream, then finish with chocolate leaves.

Sherry Pear Trifle

Base
1 chocolate swiss roll, sliced
400g (14oz) can pear halves, drained
150ml (¼ pint) sweet sherry

Custard
1½ tablespoons custard powder
1 tablespoon caster sugar
600ml (1 pint) milk
115g (4oz) plain Scotbloc or Chocolat,
grated

Decoration
150ml (¼ pint) whipped cream
2 tablespoons flaked almonds, toasted
Scotts Real Chocolate Leaves
glacé cherry

1 Arrange slices of swiss roll in serving dish. Reserve two pair halves. Cut remainder into pieces and place in bowl. Pour on sherry and leave to soak for 30 minutes.

2 Blend custard powder and sugar with 3 tablespoons of milk. Heat remainder of milk with the chocolate until melted. Pour onto blended powder and boil until thick.

3 Cool custard slightly and pour over the base. Leave to set. When cold, decorate as shown.

Meringue and Chocolate Layer Gateau

Meringue
4 egg whites, size 3
225g (8oz) caster sugar

Filling
225g (8oz) plain Scotbloc or Chocolat
6 tablespoons water
600ml (1 pint) double cream

Decoration
Scotts Real Chocolate Logs
115g (4oz) milk Scotbloc or
Chocolat, grated

1 Whisk egg whites to peaks then whisk in half the sugar. Fold in remaining sugar and pipe 3 discs onto non-stick paper. Bake at 110°C (225°F) or gas mark ¼ until dry.

2 Make filling 2-3 hours before serving. Dissolve the chocolate and water in a pan. Cool slighlty. Whip cream into peaks. Slowly add chocolate, whisk until thick.

3 Layer the meringue discs with the chocolate cream, on a serving dish. Cover top and sides then decorate with the logs and grated chocolate. Serve chilled.

Mocha Roulade

Roulade

1 tablespoon instant coffee granules

1 tablespoon warm water

115g (4oz) plain Scotbloc or Chocolat

4 large eggs, separated

115g (4oz) caster sugar

Dusting

60g (2oz) icing sugar, sieved

Filling

300ml (½ pint) double cream

1 Grease and line a 28 x 33cm (11 x 13in) swiss roll tin with greaseproof paper, then lightly grease the paper with melted butter.

2 Blend the coffee with the water to a smooth paste. Melt the chocolate in a pan over hot water then cool slightly.

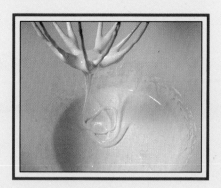

3 Whisk the egg yolks and sugar for 1 minute until light and pale in colour.

4 Using a spatula, stir the coffee and chocolate into the mixture.

5 Whisk the egg whites until stiff and lightly fold into the mixture.

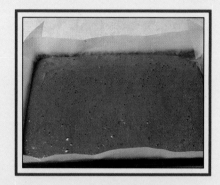

6 Spread the mixture evenly in the tin and bake at 180°C (350°F) or gas mark 4 for approximately 15 minutes.

7 When baked remove from oven and cover with a damp cloth. Leave overnight.

8 Sieve the icing sugar onto a large sheet of greaseproof paper. Upturn roulade onto the dusted surface and remove the paper (the roulade will appear moist).

9 Immediately whip cream for the filling, spread over roulade and using the greaseproof paper roll up as shown. Serve with crystallised fruit and cream.

Chocolate and Coffee Pie

Flan Case

170g (6oz) ground almonds

60g (2oz) caster sugar

1 egg white, size 3

Filling

160g (5½oz) plain Scotbloc or Chocolat

170ml (6oz) single cream

225g (8oz) cream cheese

2 tablespoons coffee liqueur

2 teaspoons powdered gelatine

2 tablespoons hot water

Decoration

whipping cream

toasted almonds

chocolate cut-outs

milk Scotbloc or Chocolat, grated

Note: Best eaten on the day it is made

1 **For the flan case:** Place the almonds, sugar and egg white into a bowl and knead to a paste. Roll into a ball. Cover and chill for 30 minutes.

2 Roll out and press into a greased 20.5cm (8in) flan dish. Bake blind at 180°C (350°F) or gas mark 4 for 25-30 minutes or until golden brown. Leave until cool.

3 **For the filling:** Melt the chocolate and cream over hot water. Do not allow to boil.

4 Cool in a refrigerator for approximately 30 minutes. Then beat the mixture until it thickens slightly.

5 Whisk in the cream cheese and liqueur. Beat until smooth.

6 Dissolve the gelatine in the hot water and stir into the chocolate mixture.

7 Spoon the mixture into the flan case. Smooth over and chill for 3-4 hours.

8 **For the decoration:** Pipe fresh cream rosettes around the edge of the flan.

9 Finish with almonds and chocolate cut-outs. Sprinkle grated chocolate in the centre.

White Chocolate Mousse

Mousse

1 level teaspoon powdered gelatine

1 tablespoon water

225g (8oz) yoghurt

170g (6oz) white Scotbloc, melted

145g (5 fluid oz) whipping cream, whipped

grated rind of 1 lemon

1 egg white, size 3

Decoration

lemon rind curls

chocolate cut-outs

serves 4

1 Dissolve the gelatine in the water. Mix the yoghurt and melted chocolate together. Stir in the melted gelatine.

2 Stir in the whipped cream and grated lemon rind.

3 Whisk the egg white and gently fold into mixture. Divide between four serving glasses. Decorate with lemon rind curls and chocolate cut-outs. Chill until required.

Chocolate Banana Pie

Base
170g (6oz) chocolate digestive biscuits
60g (2oz) butter, melted

Filling
2 small bananas
255g (9oz) condensed milk
grated rind and strained juice of 1 lemon
2 teaspoons powdered gelatine

Topping
130g (4½oz) condensed milk
115g (4oz) plain Scotbloc or Chocolat
30g (1oz) butter

Decoration
sliced banana tossed in lemon juice
whipped cream
chocolate cut-outs
white Scotbloc, grated

1 **For the base:** Crush biscuits and mix with melted butter. Press into 20.5cm (8in) flan dish. **For the filling:** Purée bananas with the condensed milk.

2 Add the lemon rind. Dissolve gelatine in juice over gentle heat then add to banana mixture. Pour into flan dish. Leave to set.

3 **For the topping:** Gently heat condensed milk, chocolate and butter and stir until melted. Cool slightly and pour over filling. Chill for at least 2 hours, then decorate.

Chocolate Custard Pots

Filling

450ml (¾ pint) milk

150ml (¼ pint) single cream

115g (4oz) plain Scotbloc or Chocolat, grated

3 eggs, size 3

1 egg yolk, size 3

30g (1oz) caster sugar

2 teaspoons rum

Decoration

whipped cream

chocolate curls

Makes 6

Note: Can be served hot or cold.

1 Heat the milk and cream in a pan with the chocolate on low temperature until just melted. Do not boil.

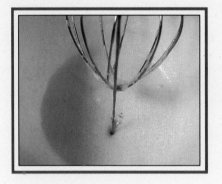

2 Whisk together the eggs, egg yolk, caster sugar and rum until a light texture is formed. Then stir in the heated chocolate mixture.

3 Strain into ovenproof serving pots placed in a tray. Half fill tray with water. Bake at 170°C (325°F) or gas mark 3 for 40 minutes. Decorate as shown.

Surprise Chocolate Mousse

Base

1 chocolate swiss roll

425g (15oz) can mandarin orange segments and juice

Mousse

225g (8oz) plain Scotbloc or Chocolat

60g (2oz) butter

4 eggs, size 3, separated

60g (2oz) marshmallows

2 tablespoons hot water or cold liqueur

Decoration

whipping cream

chopped nuts

chocolate cut-outs

mandarin orange segments

1 Slice the swiss roll and arrange in base of serving dish. Add mandarin oranges and half the juice. Melt the chocolate and butter in a basin over hot water.

2 Add egg yolks, marshmallows and hot water or liqueur and stir thoroughly until marshmallows melt and ingredients are blended.

3 Whisk egg whites until stiff and fold carefully into chocolate mixture. Pour over sponge and fruit base and leave to set. Decorate as shown.

83

Chocolate and Cream Flan

Base

225g (8oz) digestive biscuits

85g (3oz) butter, melted

Filling

2 eggs, size 3

60g (2oz) caster sugar

4 level tablespoons plain flour, sieved

115g (4oz) plain Scotbloc or Chocolat

300ml (½ pint) milk

1 tablespoon rum, optional

4 tablespoons evaporated milk

Decoration

145ml (5 fluid oz) double or whipping

cream

chocolate curls

icing sugar for dusting

serves 6-8

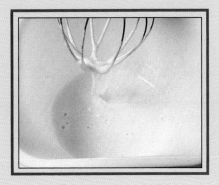

1 **For the base:** Crush the biscuits in a bowl and then mix in the melted butter. Line the base of a 23cm (9in) fluted, loose bottom flan tin with the biscuit mix.

2 **For the filling:** Whisk the eggs and sugar until thick and creamy.

3 Beat in the sieved flour until smooth.

4 Gently heat the chocolate and milk in a pan until melted. Remove from heat.

5 Immediately pour into the egg mixture. Return to pan and bring to the boil, stirring continuously.

6 Allow to cool slightly. Add the rum and lightly whisked evaporated milk.

7 Pour the mixture over the biscuit base. Place in refrigerator for 4 hours.

8 **For the decoration:** When chilled, whip the cream and spread, or pipe, over the top.

9 Place chocolate curls around the edge and centre. Dust with icing sugar, as shown.

Hot Chocolate Souffle

60g (2oz) butter, melted
60g (2oz) plain flour, sieved
300ml (½ pint) milk
70g (2½ oz) caster sugar
85g (3oz) plain Scotbloc or Chocolat,
melted
3 eggs, size 3, separated

makes 6

1 Grease ramekins with butter and dust with caster sugar.
For souffle: Mix the butter and flour, cook for 1 minute. Remove from heat and slowly beat in the milk.

2 Return to heat, bring to boil and stir to a thick paste. Remove from heat, beat in the sugar and chocolate. Cool slightly and gradually beat in the egg yolks.

3 Whisk egg whites to peaks and lightly fold into mixture. Fill ramekins, bake at 190°C (375°F) or gas mark 5 for 25-30 minutes. Dust with icing sugar and serve.

Chocolate Syllabub

Syllabub

3 tablespoons drinking chocolate powder

60ml (2 fluid oz) sweet sherry

1 tablespoon brandy

300ml (½ pint) double cream

2 egg whites, size 3

115g (4oz) plain Scotbloc or Chocolat, grated

Decoration

1 tablespoon drinking chocolate powder

wafer finger biscuits

makes 4

1 Blend the 3 tablespoons of drinking chocolate powder with the sherry and brandy, until smooth.

2 Whip the cream until it just holds its shape on the whisk, then gradually fold in the drinking chocolate mixture.

3 Whisk egg whites until peaks form, then fold into mixture with grated chocolate. Spoon into glasses. Sprinkle powder on top and serve with biscuit.

Chocolate and Ginger Cheesecake

Base

115g (4oz) plain chocolate digestive
biscuits
60g (2oz) soft brown sugar
60g (2oz) butter
85g (3oz) preserved ginger, chopped

Filling

115g (4oz) plain Scotbloc or Chocolat
225g (8oz) curd or cream cheese
115g (4oz) soft brown sugar
1 teaspoon ground ginger
Pinch of salt
2 eggs, size 3, separated
2 teaspoons powdered gelatine
3 tablespoons hot water
150ml (¼ pint) whipping cream

Decoration

whipping cream
preserved ginger
chocolate cut-outs

1 **For the base:** Crush the biscuits and place in a bowl with the sugar. Melt the butter and stir into the mixture.

2 Press the crumb mixture into a 20.5cm (8in) spring-clip cake tin. Leave to set. Sprinkle on the chopped ginger.

3 **For the filling:** Melt the chocolate. Cool slightly. Beat the cheese with 85g (3oz) of the brown sugar and stir into melted chocolate with the ginger and salt.

4 Thoroughly beat in the egg yolks one at a time.

5 Dissolve the gelatine in the hot water and stir into the mixture. Leave until almost set.

6 Whisk egg whites until stiff, then beat in the remaining brown sugar.

7 Whip the cream then fold into the chocolate mixture with alternate spoonfuls of the whisked egg whites.

8 Pour in the chocolate mixture and smooth over the surface. Chill for 3-4 hours.

9 **For decoration:** Remove from cake tin and decorate with whipped cream, ginger and chocolate cut-outs. Cover and chill until required.

Mandarin Yoghurt Dessert

Dessert

315g (11oz) can of mandarin orange segments
and juice
caster sugar to taste
30g (1oz) powdered gelatine
115g (4oz) plain Scotbloc or Chocolat
225ml (8 fluid oz) plain unsweetened yoghurt
2 tablespoons orange liqueur (optional)

Decoration

60g (2oz) whipping cream
mandarin orange segment
chocolate cut-outs

1 Drain the oranges and pour the juice into a small pan. If natural juice, add sugar to taste. Sprinkle gelatine over juice and heat gently until dissolved.

2 Melt 85g (3oz) chocolate over a pan of hot water. Gradually stir in the yoghurt, beating until smooth. Chop orange segments and stir in with the juice.

3 Grate remaining chocolate and stir in with liqueur. Pour into 600ml (1 pint) mould. Chill until set. Remove from mould and decorate.

Fudge Sauce

Sauce

150g (5¼oz) plain Scotbloc or Chocolat

130g (4½oz) marshmallows

8 tablespoons evaporated milk

1 Heat all the ingredients together in a large bowl over a pan of hot water, stirring slowly until melted.

2 The sauce can be used over ice cream, profiteroles, puddings and pies - hot or cold.

3 The sauce is ideal for dipping fresh fruits: banana, strawberry, orange etc. Leave to cool for 3 hours before dipping. Sauce can be re-heated if required.

Chocolate Muesli Delight

Filling

455g (16oz) plain yogurt
60g (2oz) unsweetened muesli
60g (2oz) hazelnuts, chopped and toasted
0225g (8oz) dried (no need to soak) apricots
2 tablespoons clear honey
115g (4oz) plain Scotbloc or Chocolat
30g (1oz) butter

Decoration

fresh whipping cream
chopped nuts

makes 4

1 **For the filling:** Mix together the yogurt, muesli and hazelnuts.

2 Roughly chop the apricots and stir into the mixture with the honey until evenly blended.

3 Melt the chocolate and butter in a separate bowl over hot water. Stir until smooth.

4 Spoon one tablespoon of yogurt mixture into each of four sundae glasses.

5 Spoon in 2 teaspoons of melted chocolate over the yogurt mixture, swirling the glass to give a thin layer.

6 Repeat steps 4 and 5, chilling between each chocolate layer.

7 Continue adding the two mixtures to create an even pattern, finishing with a layer of chocolate. Chill until set.

8 **For the decoration:** Whip the cream and pipe a rosette on top.

9 Decorate with chopped nuts and apricot pieces.

Chocolate Fruit Truffle

Truffle
455g (16oz) mixed dried fruit
4 tablespoons rum
285g (10oz) plain Scotbloc or Chocolat
115g (4oz) butter
170g (6oz) Madeira cake, crumbed
60g (2oz) icing sugar, sieved

Decoration
300ml (½ pint) whipping cream
cherries

Note: The truffle can be frozen without the cream for up to 3 months.

1 **For the truffle:** Soak the dried fruit in the rum for 2-3 hours or overnight.

2 Melt the chocolate and butter in a basin over a pan of hot water.

3 Stir the Madeira cake crumbs into the chocolate.

4 Then thoroughly stir in the fruit and icing sugar.

5 Turn the mixture into a greased 900ml (1½ pint) ring mould and press down firmly. Cover and chill until set, preferably overnight.

6 Dip the mould in hot water for 30 seconds.

7 Carefully turn the truffle out onto a serving plate.

8 **For the decoration:** Whip the cream until just thick and pour over the truffle as shown.

9 Decorate with cherries. Slice and serve.

Chocolate Boxes

Boxes
115g (4oz) white Scotbloc

Filling
mousse

ice cream

Decoration
Scotts Real Chocolate Hearts

marshmallow

fresh fruit

sponge

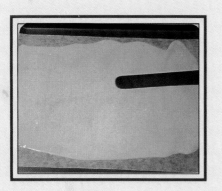

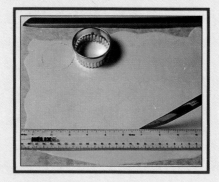

1 Melt the chocolate in a pan over hot water. Colour (see p.12) as required. Spread the chocolate thinly over greaseproof paper, using a palette knife.

2 Leave to set then cut out a 5cm (2in) wide disc and five 3cm (1¼in) squares for each box.

3 Using a small brush, fix the sides to the disc with melted chocolate. Fill as required. Place a square on top decorated with a chocolate heart.